The Banned List

The Banned List

A MANIFESTO AGAINST JARGON AND CLICHÉ

First published 2011 by Elliott and Thompson Limited
27 John Street, London WC1N 2BX
www.eandtbooks.com

ISBN: 978-1-907642-42-5

9 8 7 6 5 4 3 2 1

A CIP catalogue record for this book is available
from the British Library.

Printed and bound in the UK by CPI Group (UK) Ltd, Croydon, CR0 4YY

Typeset by PDQ

It all started with the television news and a scene familiar in homes everywhere. On 28 June 2008, I heard a political reporter for the BBC say 'It's the economy, stupid.' I don't think I shouted at the television, or threw anything, but you get the idea. No. No more. Never again. Within minutes, with the happy immediacy of the internet, I wrote: 'The phrase has been added to the list of Prohibited Clichés. By order.' I didn't have a list of Prohibited Clichés when I started writing, but, by the time I had finished, there was a list of five. The others were:

A week is a long time in politics.
What part of *x* don't you understand?

Way beyond or way more.
Any time soon.

Thus began the *Banned List*, the latest and longest version of which is before you now. It consists of more than clichés of course, because at least a cliché was shiny once, before it became dull from over-use, whereas many words and phrases have never been interesting. The list includes: pretentious words that people hope will make them look clever, or at least conceal their uncertainty; jargon intended to advertise membership of a supposedly expert order; and empty, abstract words that fill space while the writer or speaker works out what to say. They all get in the way. So here they are all laid down, never to be used again.

'It's the economy, stupid' was a particularly provoking phrase, not just because it is a cliché but because it is wrong. What James Carville, the wild and brilliant manager of Bill Clinton's 1992 presidential election campaign, wrote on the whiteboard in the war room in Little Rock,

Arkansas, was 'The economy, stupid.' It was the second of three reminders for campaign workers, the first being 'Change vs. more of the same' and the third 'Don't forget healthcare.' I am sure that photographic evidence exists somewhere, but the words were recorded by Michael Kelly, a contemporary witness, in a report for the *New York Times*, 'The 1992 Campaign: The Democrats', on 31 October 1992. (*The War Room*, a 1993 documentary in which Carville and his colleagues played themselves, also features the correct wording.)

I cannot remember what the BBC report was about, but presumably the reporter was saying that the state of the economy is a factor in politics. This is not always true. The recession did for George Bush Sr in 1992, but not for John Major a few months earlier. The assertion requires evidence and explanation. Instead, all we got was a phrase so memorable that everyone misremembers it. This was television, a stultifying medium, and the reporter had to come to a conclusion in under two and a half minutes.

At least the phrase was pungent once, even though it began to go stale in about 1993. It finally crumbled to dust when it was adopted by the Green Party in 2009 as the title of its manifesto for the European elections, *it's the economy, stupid*, which used the typographical device of putting the whole thing in lower case that had been fashionable in the 1980s.

Some clichés disappear eventually, and this may be one of them. It seems to be on the wane, although it has already lasted nearly two decades. 'A week is a long time in politics' has lasted nearly thirty years longer. It is even less authentic. At least part of 'it's the economy, stupid' is genuine. The legend of Harold Wilson's cliché is that he said it to lobby journalists around 1964, but no one wrote it down at the time. Nigel Rees, author of *Sayings of the Century*, asked Wilson in 1977, and he could not recall when or even whether he had said it.

The phrase may owe its durability to it meaning even less than 'the economy, stupid'. All it means is 'stuff happens'. In this it is curiously similar to 'events, dear boy, events', another unverifiable cliché-quotation from the time, attributed to another prime minister called Harold. Alastair Horne, Macmillan's biographer, told Robert Harris that he thought his subject might have been referring to the Profumo affair, which was in 1963, but the phrase was not recorded (as 'attributed') by the *Oxford Dictionary of Quotations* until 1999.

We do not know who Macmillan's 'dear boy' was, or what his question had been, although the gist suggests itself. Yet Wilson's cliché is even more persistent, perhaps because it can be varied so easily. 'If a week is a long time in politics, then a month is an eternity', or 'an hour is now a long time in politics'. The most ingenious recent variation was by Mark Field, the Conservative MP, in an article in 2010. Writing about parliamentary boundaries that would not be decided for another three years, he concluded: 'And as we know 156 weeks is a long time in politics …'

Other clichés are intensely but briefly fashionable. 'What part of *x* don't you understand?' is defunct already. It was popular in the British press around the middle of 2008. Alice Miles, the *Times* columnist, had just used it to brutally dismissive effect in April, when interest rates were rising and some homeowners complained about market forces as if Margaret Thatcher had never existed: 'Coming to the end of a fixed-rate deal? Tough. What part of Two-Year Fixed Rate didn't you understand?' The economy changed in September — interest rates went down after the collapse of Lehman Bros — but the phrase itself was already cold ash. I have not seen it in print for years, although a search of an electronic database of national newspapers reveals a notably lame use in March 2011: 'The coalition promised "respect" to Scotland. What part of that word don't they understand?' But that was in the Scottish edition of *The Express*, so it hardly counts.

The use of 'way' instead of 'far' is a different kind of cliché: that of the over-use in serious writing of a young person's style of speech. When variations of slang are first used they can tickle the pleasure of recognition — assuming the slang is well known enough — or of simple novelty, but the trick works only once or twice. Usage can change, we all know that, but it is better for the writer not to be the abrasive edge that wears down the reader's resistance. One day, 'way' may be accepted as an alternative to 'far', but let second-rate writers achieve that if the market will bear it.

No such defence can be mounted for 'any time soon', even if its initial attraction was similar, as a compliment paid by the old — or the old country — to the young. The adoption by British writers of Americanisms follows the same cycle of freshness, irritation and selective acceptance, but 'any time soon' is not a different way of saying 'soon', just a longer one.

The Banned List actually started as an email, now lost, that I wrote around 2000 with some rules for leading articles in *The Independent*. They should never begin with 'So', I said. Since then I have realised that this is only the first of a rising three-part scale. Worse is to start an article with 'And so'. Worst of all is 'And so it begins.' Time can be saved by not reading on if an article starts with any of those. Although that kind of sweeping judgement can lead one astray, as it once did Martin Amis, to whom I shall come in a moment.

Most of my other rules were more specific to leading articles. (I said we should use formal language such as 'leading article' rather than 'leader', 'newspaper' rather than 'paper' and avoid contractions such as 'don't' and 'can't'; the other rule that I remember was: 'We never call for a debate, because we know what we think.') The guidelines also advised against the use of foreign languages, as did George Orwell, to whom I shall also come in a moment, or dead ones, which Orwell did not mention. I think there had been some debate in the office about the use of the Latin word *pace*, in which it turned out that some people not only did not know what it means ('with respect to' in the sense of 'contrary to the opinion of') but thought that it is a way of citing someone in one's support. *Quod erat demonstrandum.*

It would be a cliché, and wrong, to say that I was standing on the shoulders of giants in compiling those guidelines, and this List. I am not standing on anything; I am stealing. It was Henry Fowler whom I burgled first. His *Modern English Usage* is a fine browsing-ground for those who care about clear writing, although, as David Crystal points out in his introduction to the 2009 reissue of the first edition, Fowler contradicts himself repeatedly. People who object that 'under the circumstances' ought to be 'in the circumstances' (a good point, now he mentions it) are dismissed as 'puerile'. He says that using the prefix 'super-' not in its primary sense of 'above' or 'transcending' but meaning 'of a superior kind', 'as in superman, supermarket, superministry … is so evidently convenient that it is vain to protest when others indulge in it' (a lovely condescension).

But, as Crystal notes, 'when Fowler encounters a usage he does not like, his language alters'. For example, he refuses to tolerate the coming together of 'forceful' and 'forcible' — 'such writers injure the language' — and he condemns the use of 'phenomenal' to mean 'remarkable' as having had 'unreasonable vogue'. He says that 'believers in sound English may deliver their attack upon such usages with hope of success'. How wrong he turned out to be.

Then came George Orwell, whom I admire mainly because his real name was Blair.

Others admire him because he wrote well and passionately against sloppy political writing. Not that his own writing is universally praised. According to Christopher Hitchens, Martin Amis 'declined to go any further into *Nineteen Eighty-Four* because the words "ruggedly handsome features" appear on the first page'. (The features belong to Big Brother in a poster.) Amis said: 'The man can't write worth a damn.' Hitchens tells the story in his memoir, *Hitch-22*, and Amis confirmed it to Michael Ezra, a friend of mine. Amis would 'never let friendship take precedence over his first love, which was and is the English language', wrote Hitchens, who admitted that his friend had once rebuked him for using 'no mean achievement' in an article. I have added that to the List too.

Amis later grudgingly admitted that *Nineteen Eighty-Four* improved after its unfortunate start, but Orwell is cited here because he compiled an early version of the Banned List in his essay, 'Politics and the English Language', in 1946.

He identified four categories of verbiage: 'dying metaphors, verbal false limbs, pretentious diction and meaningless words'.

His examples of dying metaphors were:

> Ring the changes on, take up the cudgel for, toe the line, ride roughshod over, stand shoulder to shoulder with, play into the hands of, no axe to grind, grist to the mill, fishing in troubled waters, on the order of the day, Achilles' heel, swan song, hotbed.

All of them I have added to my list, except 'fishing in troubled waters', which is now extinct. I thought that 'take up the cudgel for' was sleeping with the fishes too, but I found that Jemima Khan had stepped outside her Oxfordshire mansion to 'take up the cudgels for human rights', according to my good colleague Ian Burrell of *The Independent* in December 2010. The pluralisation of the original cudgel is one of those subtle changes that clichés undergo over decades. The 'on the' has dropped off 'the order of the day', and 'toe the line' has been rendered so featureless by over-use that it is now often written as 'tow the line', which is a different metaphor altogether.

'Verbal false limbs' was hardly an elegant phrase, but you see what Orwell meant when he explained:

> Characteristic phrases are render inoperative, militate against, make contact with, be subjected to, give rise to, give grounds for, have the effect of, play a leading part (role) in, make itself felt, take effect, exhibit a tendency to, serve the purpose of.

I have added them all. They are all still current, although some are more offensive than others. ('Militate against' is a particular menace because some people confuse 'militate' and 'mitigate', which turns it into a nonsense phrase.)

When he came to 'pretentious diction' Orwell

seems to have run out of time to think of really objectionable examples.

> Words like phenomenon, element, individual (as noun), objective, categorical, effective, virtual, basic, primary, promote, constitute, exhibit, exploit, utilise, eliminate, liquidate.

Many of them are unattractive and should be substituted by shorter, more direct words if possible, but 'element', 'primary' and 'exploit' are perfectly good words of precise meaning.

Others of his examples may have evolved since 1946. It would be fussy to rule against the use of individual as a noun now. But most of them are objectionable only if misused. 'Promote' and 'constitute' are useful words in the right places and are pretentious only if used to mean 'encourage' or 'make up'. So I have not added these, except 'utilise', which has no place in the English language as long as the 'tili' can be excised.

Orwell's examples of meaningless words — class, totalitarian, science, progressive, reactionary, bourgeois, equality — also seem unnecessarily argumentative. What he means is that they are often used to add value judgements surreptitiously to statements about which the reader ought to be allowed to make up his or her own mind. Again, most of them cannot be banned altogether, and even 'progressive', which is on my Banned List, is permitted when making an arithmetical point about tax systems.

Orwell's essay also set out six flawed rules to help write good English:

1. Never use a metaphor, simile, or other figure of speech which you are used to seeing in print.
2. Never use a long word where a short one will do.
3. If it is possible to cut a word out, always cut it out.
4. Never use the passive where you can use the active.

5. Never use a foreign phrase, a scientific word, or a jargon word if you can think of an everyday English equivalent.
6. Break any of these rules sooner than say anything outright barbarous.

The first and the fifth are all right, but the others depend on the sixth to make sense of their ironic absolutism. It may be possible *never* to use foreign, scientific or jargon words, but not even Martin Amis could abide by the first rule all the time. Criticising Orwell for his 'never' and 'always' might seem a bit rich — or even, to test rule five, a case of lese-majesty[*] — from someone who has called his own book *The Banned List*. But it would have been more use if Orwell had said a bit more about the reasons for going against his rules than the avoidance of the 'outright barbarous'.

Barbarity is not the test. Sometimes long words are more interesting than short ones. Sometimes

---

[*] Lese-majesty is actually an Anglicised phrase; the French is *lèse majesté*.

words that are strictly superfluous improve the rhythm of a sentence, or make it funny. The common complaint against sub-editors is that the first thing they do is take out all the jokes. It is possible to cut them out, so if the article is too long they do so. (Although the complaint is often unfair: if a sub-editor takes out a joke, the first possibility that ought to be considered is that *it was not funny*.)

And where would you stop? It would be *possible* to cut out all but the first paragraph of most news stories, and some media organisations seem to aspire to this model. William Shakespeare could have written, 'boy meets girl and everyone dies', but the play would have lacked a certain 'I know not what', as the French say. Or we could all write nothing at all and abandon what Erich Fromm called the struggle against pointlessness. Rule four is an exaggeration too. Sometimes, if only to vary the mood, the passive is to be preferred (I cannot say it, because it is on the List, but if you *did* see what I did there, well done).

With those qualifications, then, Orwell's rules are all very well, but we are particularly interested here in his lists of examples. They are one of the sources on which I have drawn in compiling the Banned List.

Some of the List was put together from my chance dislikes that, like that stupid economy, caused me to sublimate my desire to shout at the radio or television, or to throw down a newspaper in disgust. Increasingly, others nominated their own dislikes for inclusion, which I accepted or rejected with arbitrary power. Readers of my blog and other Twitter users were my best resource. Contrary to Google's being 'white bread of the mind', in the loopy phrase of Tara Brabazon, a professor of media studies at Brighton University, the power of computers can be harnessed for mutual self-improvement. Yes, there is a lot of text-message abbreviation on the internet, a lot of carelessly-written comment and a lot of badly-written pretension. But there is also a lot of good writing, a freshness of expression and all kinds of new slang, some of which is highly inventive and ticklish.

The internet can allow people to dumb down, if that is what they want, but it is also a liberator for those seeking out quality. My experience is that people care about language; pedantry is also popular. The internet is not destroying the language but giving us new ways of shaming its most prominent practitioners into using it better.

Suggestions from people online now make up most of the List, and their contributions reveal that there is a core of linguistic crimes that causes most offence. 'Going forward' is possibly the current top irritant. 'Around' to mean about, as in 'address issues around gender', 'iconic' and 'no brainer' are persistently nominated. Then there are the vogue phrases of commentary, especially political commentary, and especially those borrowed from business jargon, such as 'the elephant in the room', 'perfect storm', 'parameter' and 'pressing all the right buttons'. This core changes over time – as I have noted, some clichés go through a cycle like diseases: outbreak, spread, peak and decline. Sometimes they become part of the language, as if the ectoplasm of English has absorbed the infection and turned it to useful purpose. There has been a fashion that has lasted for some years, for example, for 'verbing' nouns: access, impact, foreground and address.

Some readers directed my attention to lists other than Orwell's that someone else had prepared earlier. Matthew Parris and Paul Flynn made a list called 'Political Deadspeak' for a BBC Radio 4 programme called *Not My Words, Mr Speaker* in September 2007. It had 'dialogue of the deaf', 'economics of the madhouse', 'not rocket science', 'level playing field', 'siren voices' and many more that I have copied and pasted.

Allan Christiansen, an official at Auckland Council in New Zealand, sent me a list of his translations of bureaucratic jargon, which included:

Action point: Place where you go for some action. Pub, nightclub, etc.

Enhancement meeting: Hair appointment,
    facial, makeover or any other beauty
    treatment that looks great for five
    minutes and then reverts to its old self.
Hot desk: Stolen.
Work-flowed: The result of quickly lifting
    up your desk at one end. Also known as
    a planned-slide, or clear desk policy.
Workstreams: Office flood.

Some of his suggestions are on the list, although
the imaginary Committee ruled that the examples above were peculiar to large organisations
and have not (yet) seeped into general use.

Graydon Carter, the editor of *Vanity Fair*,
had a short list of journalese words, which his
writers were not allowed to use. It included
opine, pen (as a verb) and inadvisable alternatives to 'said' (chortled, joked, quipped), which
I adopted, as well as injunctions against the use
of funky, glitz and weird, which I did not.

One of the words on Carter's list was
'plethora', which needs no further explanation

but is so much more interesting if it gets it. Like so many of the worst items on the list it is not only a cliché but it is usually used incorrectly. This was best explained by my learned colleague Guy Keleny:

> Do we really need a word that means a harmful excess of something which, in due measure, would be beneficial? Yes, actually, we do; and that is what 'plethora' means. If we keep using it to mean just 'a lot', then we will lose a useful word, which would be a pity. [*The Independent*, 28 May 2011.]

Too late now, I suspect. But Guy's 'Errors & Omissions' column in *The Independent* (it used to be called 'Mea Culpa', which was not strictly accurate and not English but I rather liked it) was one of my best sources for the Banned List. He not only identified candidates for inclusion, but drily explained why they are so objectionable.

It was he who identified a new genus of waffle: 'those terms ending in "of" that amount to little more than preliminary throat-clearing.' They include 'the level of', 'a sense of', 'a series of', 'the introduction of', 'a package of', 'a basket of', 'a raft of', 'a range of' and 'the prospect of'. As he said, 'They can nearly always be struck out.' [*The Independent*, 30 October 2010.] In one sweeping movement, he added nine items to the list. 'All the hallmarks of' makes it ten, and Liz Kendall, the MP for Leicester West and a former adviser at the Department of Health, added 'a suite of' policies, a phrase that she said was 'beloved' there.

Thus my list grew. Sometimes it felt as if it had grown too long. Some of my correspondents complained that it would be easier to publish a list of words and phrases that are permitted, or that I was trying to reduce all communication to grunts and clicks. This is untrue: English is such a rich language that, no matter how long the Banned List becomes, the scope for creativity and originality with what is left remains infinite. It would be hard, and beside the point, however, to list *all* the figures of speech 'which you are used to seeing in print'.

The List is not in the business of simply compiling over-used metaphors, archaisms and jargon; it is a selection of the most irritating. Common or garden clichés are therefore permitted. Their main interest — and it is not *that* interesting — lies in their origins. The earliest use of 'common or garden' identified by the *Oxford English Dictionary* was in a 1657 botany book: 'The Common or Garden Nightshade is not dangerous.'

Provided that they keep themselves to themselves, that they are not trying to annoy, plain clichés may be waved through on a temporary idiom visa. The scales falling from the eyes (that was Paul, or Saul, on the road to Damascus: 'there fell from his eyes as it had been scales', *Acts* 9:18; modern translations have the less poetic but more informative 'something like fish scales fell from his eyes'); the biting of bullets (a once graphic reference to coping with pain during surgery without anaesthetic); the light at the end of the tunnel; the end game: trying to list them all starts off fun but becomes as interesting as collecting bus numbers.

Indeed, you could try to classify hackneyed words and phrases; to devise a taxonomy. There are metaphors, such as those above. There are subcategories of metaphor, such as sporting ones (playing catch-up; sticky wicket; open goal), which are bearable, because at least most people know roughly what they mean; and sub-subcategories, such as American sporting metaphors (step up to the plate; ballpark; Hail Mary pass), which are not. Nautical metaphors (on someone's watch, trimming sails, full steam ahead) are common in English, even though few people have direct knowledge of the originals. There are similes, not so common (like a rolling stone; compare thee to a summer's day; as if butter would not melt in her mouth). There are old-fashioned words (the batting of eyelids; the ploughing of furrows; the linchpin) that survived in a niche because they fitted, or because they provided variety, but which are now part of the sameness. There are new and slang words to which the same applies.

There are specialist words, and foreign words. Some of these have been assimilated and have been rendered harmless, such as cliché, French for stencil, which provides English with a word that it did not have and for which there is a need. None of these offend. Soubriquet, on the other hand, which the dictionary tells me is usually spelt sobriquet, originally meant a 'chuck under the chin', but it does not matter because we have had enough of it: it goes on the List.

The List, therefore, is not merely for clichés; it is reserved for those that grate, or that are wrong; it is for jargon so foolish that it impedes communication; and for stock devices that betray an insulting lack of thought.

WHY OH WHY OH WHY?

Why, then, do people use words that count against them? There are at least three reasons: not being sure about what one is saying; wanting to be part of the in-crowd; and a lack of time.

Vagueness can be useful
First, a poor choice of words can reflect muddled thinking. Let us extract three examples from the Banned List: affordable housing, social mobility and meritocracy. Each sounds as if it is a good thing that requires no further explanation or argument. Thus the writer or speaker zooms on to the next point, without realising that what they have said is either meaningless

or contentious. The reader or listener, meanwhile, will either nod along or mutter, 'wait a moment', depending on whether they agree with the author's general political outlook, but will be none the wiser.

Affordable housing — affordable anything — is a concept ripe with assumptions. At its simplest, it means housing that the person-to-be-housed can afford. But it is never used simply to describe the housing market as it is. It means homes, usually for rent, at below-market prices. It therefore implies interfering with supply or demand. Usually it means that one group of people — taxpayers — subsidise rents for a target group defined by some quality that makes them worthy of public generosity. Sometimes this target group is defined by other words on the List: key workers, or members of this or that community. This suggests further uncertainty about meaning, and distracts attention from the next questions, which might be: How should the beneficiaries be decided? What effect does this have on incentives? Are there better ways of achieving the ends of the policy?

Social mobility is similarly ambiguous. Its first apparent meaning is a society in which children from poor families can, if talented and hard-working, achieve wealth and status. America is often believed to be such a society, not least by its own citizens, although it is that belief rather than the actual ease of upward mobility that seems to give the country its spirit. In its pure sense, a socially mobile society must be one in which it is easy to move down the social scale as well as up, which is not what people usually mean. If it simply means a society in which the middle class is expanding (that is, in which a lot of people move from the working class to the middle class in the course of their lives) then it does not mean much.

Meritocracy is a different case, because it is a word invented to contradict the sense in which it is now commonly used. It is normally used as if it were a desirable state of affairs, although it originally described a vision of an unpleasant future. *The Rise of the Meritocracy* was the title of a book by Michael Young (father of Toby and author of Labour's 1945 manifesto), published in 1958. Set in 2033, it is a parable of a ruling class chosen on narrowly-defined merit, which therefore thinks it is morally superior to those not selected.

These examples took hold because they sounded better than their alternatives: subsidised housing, equal opportunity (itself a hackneyed and ambiguous phrase) and selection or appointment on merit. They sounded good and skated over hard problems. They enjoyed a vogue, and then settled like a layer of sediment in the dialect of social policy writers and politicians.

They are notable examples of the hundreds of words and phrases that are used to cover up lack of thought or uncertainty of meaning. Some of them seem so silly that their survival needs explanation. Take 'the exception that proves the rule', the first half of an old legal maxim that goes on: 'in cases not excepted'. It means that if a sign says 'No entry on Thursdays' (the exception) it may be assumed that entry is permitted on other days (the rule). Yet the phrase is usually used to mean that something (a tabby cat) that fails to conform to a rule (all cats are black) proves that the rule is right. Which is absurd, yet it survives because it is a reflex way of trying to brush aside evidence that does not fit.

Most muddle-words, though, are just idle. Words such as 'prioritise' and 'proactive' are used to suggest vigour without troubling anyone with choices that might have to be made.

Management jargon words are the worst: 'time horizons', 'synergy' and 'thinking outside the box' cannot be contradicted, because you do not have to be sure what you mean yourself. They are fancy ways of either saying simple things, or saying nothing much at all. In their waves they too became fashionable and settled at the bottom of the stream of language, and now they are used in the vain hope that their fanciness will convey a dynamism or sophistication that the writer or speaker fears is lacking. Instead, their use all too often confirms those fears.

One example will suffice. Baroness Buscombe, chair of the Press Complaints Commission, said on the day that the *News of the World* closed: 'The reality is this is an opportunity for us to say "time out" – we've got to move on, we've got to get some good out of this.'[†] That was two common or garden clichés followed by two banned phrases. 'The reality is' is standard thinking-time verbiage, and 'opportunity' is a way of saying 'chance' in five syllables instead of one. 'Time out' is subject to a blanket ban on American sporting metaphors: here it seems to mean that 'we' should pause to take stock. And moving on is what people try to do – usually after they have drawn a line in the sand – when they want to change the subject. So all she said, once the fashionable fancy-speak was cleared away, was that we have to get some good out of this, which can be filed under pious hopes.

[†] Anthony Bramley-Harker wrote a letter to *The Independent* on 11 July 2011 to suggest that Lady Buscombe 'ought to be able to express herself in clearer and more original language than this'.

Fitting in with the in-crowd

Fashion is the second of my three explanations for the over-use of certain words or phrases. I can remember how words and phrases, especially swear words, became fashionable at school, and would spread through a year-group, quickly becoming so prevalent that most pupils would cease to realise that they were using them. Then new words would replace them and the old ones would cling on at the margins or die out altogether. The same thing happens to grown-ups.

'Going forward' must have once – and only once – seemed an original way of implying that some plan had a bit of momentum. 'Ownership' must have once seemed a new way of saying that customers or clients should be given the impression that they have a choice. A 'silo' must have once seemed a vivid metaphor for a department cut off from other parts of an organisation. So they were copied in bureaucracies, just as 'in' phrases and words are in the playground. Bureaucracies create their own subcultures, of which jargon is an important part. Junior staff copy senior staff, often in an unconscious attempt to ingratiate themselves, and before you know it the staff who deal with the general public are calling us stakeholders and telling us that there are ongoing issues around accessing the interface.

The vogue words are membership badges for the club. Sometimes the members share a genuine expertise, such as in financial markets. Phrases such as 'wall of money', 'take a haircut' or 'deleverage' mark out members of this elite, but are quickly copied by financial journalists and sometimes spread, by analogy and metaphor, to the rest of us.

The club does not have to share any special knowledge, though. These days vogue phrases often start on the internet. The vitality and informality of online comments and conversation have enriched the language, and that means that some of the most popular formulations become over-used. 'You couldn't make it up' was once a fresh and breezy way of saying that something was surprising. The use *for effect* of casual oral language, such as, 'but hey', 'ahem' or 'end of' once *had* an effect.

When the first person put full stops after every word, it must have made the point. Or the full point. Later, Christopher Hitchens adapted the technique to relate what Kingsley Amis said of Graham Greene's novel, *The Human Factor*, when it was published in 1978: 'Absolutely no. Bloody good. AT ALL!' It was all very well the Hitch doing it in a book in 2010, but you have had your fun, and now the use of full stops for emphasis. Has. Got. To. Stop. AND THE SAME GOES FOR CAPITALS.

Once mannerisms have become embedded in the language, it requires an effort to avoid them. By the same osmosis that works in school, presumably the same social instinct by which language and group identities have evolved, we copy the verbal markers of our peers. But once the freshness has worn off, they become 'herd words and herd phrases', as Kingsley's son Martin called them.

The allure of the easy cliché
Thus we come to the third reason why the verbiage gets through: lack of time. Sometimes this is laziness; sometimes a calculation that it is not worth the trouble; sometimes there really is no time. Some of the worst offences against the language tend to be oral, because, unless you are one of those rare beings who speak in complete paragraphs, you do not have time to go back and edit.

Heidi Corbally, one of my correspondents, said that 'I'm not going to lie', mostly a tic of the spoken word, was her biggest bugbear, before realising that bugbear is also a cliché. 'D'oh!' she said. Which is also on the List, although there are disputes about its spelling. Bugbear, though, is one of those more interesting clichés, because it has changed meaning. It used to be a bogey-bear, a creature in the form of a bear invented to frighten children and therefore an object of irrational fear. Because of the slang meaning of 'bug', it has come to mean an irritant.

It is because of the press of time that journalists and politicians are so often offenders against the language. Journalists because they are sometimes up against a deadline; politicians because they do so much talking and, when their speeches are written down, they are often written in a hurry. It is when you do not have time that you take a metaphor within easy reach and rush on, without pausing to think about what it means or to form a picture in your mind of what you have said. That is how we come across that quarry of truffle-hunting pedants, the mixed metaphor. No newspaper can avoid them: even *The Independent* has published these headlines in recent years: 'Domino effect could trigger meltdown'; 'Obama in last-ditch dash to stave off Democratic defeat'; 'Ahmadinejad wields axe to cement his position.'

It is because they are short of time that politicians call any alleged shortfall in opponents' funding plans a 'black hole' (a mass so dense and with gravity so strong that not even light can escape), any policy that they think is not going to work a 'car crash' (often a 'car crash waiting to happen' or happening 'in slow motion') or any trait something that is in someone's DNA. That is why the opposition is always guilty of breathtaking hypocrisy. Or rank hypocrisy. Or breathtaking arrogance.

The more important politicians do not even have time to write their own speeches, and they thus suffer verbiage syndrome by proxy. Nick Clegg is a terrible offender except when Richard Reeves is drafting his material. Tony Blair used to speak fluent cliché. I can quote his unintentional self-parody from memory: 'A day like today is not a day for sound bites really, we can leave those at home, but I feel the hand of history upon our shoulder with respect to this, I really do.' (On arriving in Belfast, 7 April 1998.) But he had good speech writers – Alastair Campbell, Peter Hyman and Phil Collins – and could read their less hackneyed material with equal conviction.

It is surprising how cliché-ridden some of David Cameron's speeches are. His announcement of the partial retreat on health service reform in June 2011 was alarming. 'Pillar to post.' 'In the driving seat.' 'Frontline.' 'Level playing field.' 'Cherry picking.' 'Sticking with the status quo is not an option.' 'A National Health Service not a National Sickness Service.' 'One-size-fits-all.' 'Reinvent the wheel.' 'Let me be absolutely clear.' 'No ifs or buts.'

Some of Ed Miliband's speeches are commendably cliché-free; yet others consist almost entirely of the tired metaphors and meaningless abstractions of a style so familiar on the left. The Labour leader made a speech around the time of Cameron's health service compendium that was just as clichéd, only they were distinctively left-wing clichés. He said that Labour needs to 'own the future', and this was how he proposed to do it: 'In the future the Labour offer to aspirational voters must be that we will address the new inequality by hard wiring fairness into the economy.'

See what I mean?

Some politicians, though, are on the side of clarity of expression. It was James Purnell, former Secretary of State for Work and Pensions, who wrote to me in April 2010: '*Please* can we ban "elephants in the room" in "perfect storms" who "seal the deal"? Please.' I was happy to oblige, but being on the right side of *that* cause had not saved him, however, for the greater Cause (he resigned from the Cabinet in June 2009, possibly in protest at Gordon Brown's repeated use of the phrase 'meet and master' when referring to the challenges of the 21st century). It may be that politicians who care about English spend more time than is good for them taking out herd words from what civil servants write for them when they should be organising to change party leader.

Chris Mullin, for example, had a feel for language and a strong sense of the ridiculous. (I first met him in 1981, when he — as well as being Tony Benn's emissary on Earth — was chairman of the Vassal ward Labour Party in Vauxhall, and I, as a new member engaged in displacement activity, tried to correct the grammar of some leftist motion; amused by my naivety, he accepted my amendment.) Here is the entry for 21 December 1999 in his diary as a junior minister:

> Keith Hill [later Tony Blair's parliamentary private secretary] and I amused ourselves compiling a New Labour lexicon. We came up with the following: pathfinders, beacons, win-win, stakeholders, opportunities as well as challenges, joined-up government, partnership, best value. These words increasingly crop up in official submissions. I am forever deleting them. 'Taking forward' is one of my favourites. It usually means doing nothing.

Some politicians try to stop guff being drafted for them but find that they cannot hold the line, not even if, like Mullin, they have the advantage of a journalist's experience. Michael Gove, a fine columnist on *The Times*, did what any incoming minister with any feeling for words would have done when he became Education Secretary in

2010. He banned some of the managerial jargon with which his department had become infected — so badly that its name had been triadised: it had been called the Department for Children, Schools and Families for three years.

Gove's memo, leaked in August 2010, tried to abolish jargon — but mostly replaced it with new nonsense. 'Targets and outcomes' became 'Results and impact'. 'Integrated working' became 'People working better to provide better services'. 'Safeguarding' became 'Child protection' (that one was all right). 'Family Intervention Projects' became 'Key workers providing intensive support to families'.

Oh well. At least he tried. Too many politicians do not even make the effort, and too many of the journalists who write about them do so in a prose style in which the turns of phrase are so predictable that the reader can finish their sentences for them.

Brian O'Nolan satirised this kind of writing under the pen name Myles na Gopaleen in *The Irish Times* until his death in 1966. The Myles na Gopaleen Catechism of Cliché was a call-and-response game:

What is a bad thing worse than? Useless.
What can one do with fierce
    resistance? Offer it.
But if one puts fierce resistance, in what
    direction does one put it? Up.
What does pandemonium
    do? It breaks loose.
Describe its subsequent dominion. It reigns.

This could be kept up for some time, and it was: 'When things are few, what also are they? Far between.' I have added that to the list.

What are stocks of fuel doing when
    they are low? Running.
How low are they running? Dangerously.
What does one do with a sugges-
    tion? One throws it out.
For what does one throw a suggestion
    out? For what it may be worth.

Anyone can join in. Try it yourself. What are guarantees made from? Cast iron. With what are they bottomed? Copper. And what are they not worth? The paper they are written on.

The predictability of some phrases has become so time-worn that parts of them exist only in stock pairs. Bated, scot, knell and squib are now used only in familiar pairs. Use of these words is expressly permitted, provided that they are detached from their siblings.

'HOW TO BE TOPP'

The title of the second volume of Geoffrey Willans and Ronald Searle's work of genius announces the intention of Molesworth, the 'goriller of 3B', to give advice to his fellow wets, oiks, snekes, bulies and cads on how to Sukceed at skool. My aim here is similar. The reason to avoid clichés is not because a smart alec might point them out and make fun of you. As Peter Victor, the news editor of *The Independent on Sunday*, once told me, 'Nobody likes a smart alec' (I think it was 'alec'), and I have tried to live my life by the light of his wisdom since. No, I am here to help. The reason to avoid clichés is that so doing is the secret of being Topp.

You may ask: Why should anyone care if a minority of pedants and pettifogeys want to ban words and phrases whose meaning is clear? I hope I have begun to explain that I am not concerned for my own tender sensibility. On the contrary, my only concern is your self-interest. I am assuming that you, the reader, on occasion write things. Or speak. And I want to pass on to you a tip. Well, a number of tips, obviously, which is why there is a long list at the back. But one meta-tip, of which the List is merely the mechanical elaboration. Which is that if you avoid over-used, pretentious and abstract phrases — if you avoid annoying or boring the reader or listener — *people will think that you are cleverer than you actually are.*

This is the opposite of the natural instinct to think that, in order to impress, we should use language that is intended to be impressive. Hence the mania for long words, grand abstractions and jargon designed to advertise membership of a specialist elite. They are all counter-productive. As readers and listeners, we admire someone who is clear and to the point, but as writers and speakers, we are too often embarrassed by simplicity, fearing that it might expose the thinness of what we have to say. My purpose here is to try to counter that instinct: to recall that, however small an idea, it always seems more impressive if it is simply expressed.

This can be illustrated by what may seem a separate point, about pedantry. The reason why pedantry matters is not because the 'correct' spelling, grammar or point of detail is superior to a form that has often been decided arbitrarily by unknown authority. It matters because enough people notice such things, and it affects how they evaluate a piece of writing. I have noticed that, if I use formal grammar, readers tend to think that what I have said is well-informed and perceptive, even if it is the same old Blairite rubbish.

This has been demonstrated by Google, which now rates the spelling and grammar of web pages to help it rank the trustworthiness and 'quality' of sites. Clichés and jargon are like spelling mistakes or grammatical errors: they are markers of poor quality. Unclear expression may not actually betray muddled thinking, as the old school say, but people think it does, and that is what matters. Verbiage, or its absence, influences your unconscious Google ranking system.

Since I am addressing you directly, I should say something about you, because getting 'the reader' right is the starting point of good writing. Or, at least, the wrong idea of 'the reader' in the writer's mind can encourage hackneyed, pretentious and abstract writing. Guy Keleny put it thus:

> It is easy for writers to picture their readers as a big group of people, a sort of public meeting taking place on some plane of the imagination. Maybe some readers like to think of themselves as members of a cosy club, and certainly some publications play up to the idea by addressing their readers in the second person plural. But it is all a fiction. The

'readers' may be many, but they never meet as a body or form a community. The lived experience is that of a single person, reading a book, a newspaper or a screen. I shall continue to think of you, dear reader, as the one person you actually are. [*The Independent*, 11 December 2010.]

Christopher Hitchens, as ever, managed to elaborate, brilliantly, and with reference to himself:

The most satisfying compliment a reader can pay is to tell me that he or she feels personally addressed. Think of your own favorite authors and see if that isn't precisely one of the things that engage you, often at first without your noticing it. A good conversation is the only human equivalent: the realising that decent points are being made and understood, that irony is in play, and elaboration, and that a dull or obvious remark would be almost physically hurtful. [*Vanity Fair*, June 2011.]

That is the test. The writer or speaker may think, 'It'll do; my meaning is clear enough,' but that is not enough. Most readers or listeners may not notice or care that a figure of speech is 'dull or obvious', but if a minority is put off, you are restricting yourself needlessly. Worse, that minority is a leading indicator. If some are repelled, more will be bored. Clarity, brevity and originality are rewarded, even if the audience is not aware of them.

If you write 'way beyond' or 'way more', most of your readers may not notice. A few others may notice, even subliminally, and think that you are a happening dude. And a few old fogeys may notice and may twitch, possibly also subliminally, with irritation. We may be morally wrong to do so, but it is too late now.

The damage has been done, and you cannot go back and argue the point. The damage is greater, sadly, than any kudos that may have been earned by using the fashionable jargon of the in-crowd. So you carry on, talking about flatlining because the interface is unfit for purpose, and each jargon word or phrase alienates another sliver of your audience while failing, because they are so familiar, to excite the interest of people who recognise that they share the language of the privileged group.

It is no use, as I hope I have demonstrated, saying that 'exponential' has come to be accepted as meaning 'fast' or 'big' rather than a logarithmic change. Or pointing out that Chambers includes 'very rapidly' as a definition of 'exponentially'. It is a dictionary; it describes language as it is used. This includes the misuse of many other words from mathematics and science, such as parameter (which is often used to mean boundary, by confusion with perimeter, rather than a constant that may change) and quantum leap (which is a change of state in an electron and therefore very small).

It is no use, in other words, saying that *most people* use words to mean something that they did not originally mean, or even that *everyone* understands perfectly well what is meant by them. Both of those are true, but irrelevant. If there is a large enough minority in your audience who will be distracted, confused or irritated by what they consider to be incorrect usage, you have conceded an advantage needlessly.

So you know what to do. Remember George Orwell's 'ruggedly handsome features' and his failure to write by his own rules. It helps to recall his most important rule, as well as to note that it is observed by approximation rather than tyranny: Try not to use figures of speech that you are used to seeing in print. Just take them out. The worst that can happen is that you make the opposite mistake, of trying too hard to think of fresh similes or metaphors, which read oddly and distract the reader from what is being said. Or of spending too long trying to think of new ways of expressing a simple thought.

Never worry about a piece of writing being too short. This is a rare failing, and one to be sought rather than avoided. (How often do you say, 'Did it have to end so soon'?)

Prefer formal grammar, unless there is a reason for colloquialism, because informality *feels* imprecise even if the meaning is perfectly clear, and even if the reader is not aware that grammar is an issue.

Don't ignore the grammar checker without a reason — someone went to a lot of trouble to write that software, and it is right more often than the typical writer in a hurry. Indeed, whenever I have taken issue with Bill Gates's grammar I have had to concede the point to him.

Check the spellings of proper names. The computer will do the others and reading something back to yourself, aloud or in your head, may pick up mistakes that end up as correctly-spelt words.

This is not mere pedantry. True pedantry would require another book. Here we are interested only in avoiding annoying the reader. The one reader, chosen at random from the multitude, who may be the one tiresome bigot you were hoping would not be on the selection committee.

If you have something to say, better to say it simply and clearly even if you fear that it seems a little dull, or that it fails to do justice to your prowess as a writer, or to your expertise in your chosen field. The trouble starts if you realise that you do not have much to say, or that it is a mere statement of the obvious. But then at least you know where you are, which is a step ahead of those many people who have no idea at all.

The reason for caring about clear writing is not because self-appointed guardians of a questionable correctness go around trying to ban things that they think are ugly or thoughtless. It is a matter of your self-interest. If you avoid clichés and jargon people will hail you as a Sukcess. I am trying only to help. I hope you don't mind.

THE LIST

A

Above my pay grade.

Access, as a verb.

Achilles' heel.

Action, as a verb.

Added bonus (tautology).

Address, as a verb. 'Address issues' is a more
serious offence. 'Address issues around'
invites the heaviest penalty.

Affordable, especially housing. A word which
sounds as if it is obviously a good thing,
but which conceals value judgements, such
as who should pay to reduce the price, how
such a subsidy should be decided and at
what price something can be 'afforded'.

Age-old question. This is a phrase that has
 annoyed Duncan Turnbull, a correspondent
 of mine, since the dawn of time.

Agenda, except to describe a list of things to be
 discussed in a meeting.

Ahead of, to mean before.

Ahead of the curve. Or the game.

Ahem.

Aka (also known as). Incidentally, why is this
 always written in lower case, while other
 initials are in capitals? Why is it not AKA?
 As it is banned, I suppose it doesn't matter.

A-list. Or C-list. Or Z-list. Other lists are
 permitted, but won't make much sense.

All options are on the table.

And yet, and yet …

An analogue politician in a digital age, or
 variants thereof.

Any time soon.

Any way, shape or form.

Apologies for a group email asking for
 information. If people don't know, they
 press delete. You are entitled to ask. They

are entitled to ignore. It is not as if you
were a train company that has failed to
provide a service, in which case an apology is
required (and thanking passengers for their
co-operation is not).

Approbation, a longer word for 'approval'.

Arctic conditions. See conditions.

Around, used to mean about. Especially having
issues around, for example, gender. Or a
campaign around something, which is just
silly.

Art form.

Articulate, imperative verb, as in 'the leader
of the Labour Party must articulate a vision',
usually a coherent and compelling one.

As of this time.

An ask, especially 'a big ask'.

At the present time.

B

B, Plan.

Back burner.

Back in the day.

Back office.

Ballpark. This was on the Plain English
    Campaign's list of 'most annoying clichés'
    in 2004. Since then all American sporting
    metaphors have been banned. Although I
    don't mind 'fleaflicker'.

Bandied about. Bandy: pass, mention. Use
    without the 'about' is commended.

Bank of Mum and Dad.

Basis. See daily.

A basket of.

Battle lines. Do what you like with them
    except draw them, or draw them up.

Be careful what you wish for.

Be in no doubt.

Be still my beating heart. With or without
    cutesy exclamation mark.

Been there, done that, got the T-shirt.

Beleaguered, except of a city, town or fort
    with turrets.

Between a rock and a hard place.

Beyond parody, or satire.

Big beast.

Bitter battle.

Black hole, meaning that a sum does not add up.

Blame culture. See also 'culture of excuses'.

Blood and treasure.

Blood on the carpet (or floor, or walls).

Blueprint. The 19th century technology of
copying using paper coated with ferric
compounds where the bit exposed to light
turns blue could be sort of interesting. The
word is not.

Blue-sky thinking.

Boasted, to mean 'possessed' or 'featured'.

Bohemian.

Boots on the ground.

Bottom line.

Bottom-up.

Breathtaking hypocrisy. Or rank. Or
breathtaking arrogance.

A bridge too far.

Brief sojourn. A sojourn is a 'short stay',
Chambers.

By the back door.

By virtue of the fact that.

C

'We campaign in poetry. We govern in prose.'
What Mario Cuomo, Governor of New
York, actually said at Yale University, 16
February 1985, was: 'We campaign in
poetry. But when we're elected, we're forced
to govern in prose.' But it is over-used.

Campaigners, as in 'campaigners say', a
favourite of regional television news.

Capitals, use of, for emphasis. The italic font is
there for a *reason*.

Car crash (except when referring to road
accidents).

To cascade (messages, for example): one of the
worst noun-as-verb formations.

Cast-iron guarantees.

Catalogue of errors. (Does it have glossy
photographs?)

Celebrity.

Chaos, to describe roadworks, cancelled trains
or planes, or two government ministers
saying slightly different things.

Chortled (for said).

Chuckled (for said).

Civil society.

Clause Four moment.

Let's be clear. Let me be absolutely clear.

A cliché but true.

Close down discussion.

Closure. See also 'sense of'.

Coffee, the waking up and smelling thereof.

To coin a phrase.

(On a) collision course.

Comes with the territory.

Comfort zone.

(In the) coming weeks and months. 'In the
  coming period' is permitted, however,
  if referring ironically to Trotskyist analyses
  of why the revolution is just round the corner.

Community. Always suspect, so I have not
  listed separately further clichés, such as
  'close-knit', or added abstractions, such as
  'international', 'ethnic' or 'software developers'.

Compelling: not absolutely banned, but to be
  used with extreme care, or to describe the
  use or threat of force.

ConDem government.

Conditions, to mean weather.

Connect with the electorate (or reconnect with them, often by setting out a compelling agenda).

Cough up, to mean spend.

Country, as in 'up and down the'. Or 'length and breadth of the'.

Crash and burn.

Critique, as a verb.

Crowd-sourcing.

Crunch talks.

Cudgels, taking up thereof.

Culture of excuses, blame or innovation.

The cupboard is bare.

Current climate.

D

(On a) daily basis. 'Daily' or 'every day' will serve. The same principle applies to 'on a regular basis'. In fact, basis is usually suspect.

Damning or devastating indictment.

Damp squib. Dry squibs are not only
permitted but compulsory.

Dawn of time. See 'age-old question'.

Dead hand, of bureaucracy, the state, or
anything else old, heavy and a bit limp.

Dead in the water.

Dead on arrival.

Death by a thousand cuts.

Death knell.

Death of anyone or anything being greatly
exaggerated.

Deckchairs on the *Titanic*, the rearranging
thereof.

Deleverage. It means reduce debt. See
'leverage'.

Deliverables.

Demographic, as a noun.

Dialogue of the deaf.

Diarise.

Die in a ditch. Especially the last one.

Direction of travel.

Disconnect, as a noun.

Discontent, any season of.

Dislocate, as a noun. (No, I did not believe
anyone would use it either. But Paul
Mason of BBC *Newsnight* did in his blog in
November 2010: 'There is a severe dislocate
between many people and the whole
political class.')

Does what it says on the tin.

Dog whistle. The point is that only dogs can hear
them. As soon as any non-racist journalist, for
example, can detect a hidden message aimed at
racist voters, it ceases to be a dog whistle.

Doh, d'oh, der, duh: with or without
exclamation marks.

Don't hold your breath.

Downward spiral (often a spiral of decline).

DNA, as in, 'It's in his/her/their'.

Draw a line under. Or draw a line in the sand.
The thing about a line in the sand is that
it will soon be washed away by the sea. I
once heard a caller to a radio phone-in who
wanted to 'draw a line under the sand'.

Drill down.

Drive a coach and horses through.

Driver, except in a vehicle, or one of those
    things that gives you a blue-screen stop error
    on a computer when it goes wrong.
Driving seat, except in a vehicle.
Ducks, as in the ones you get in a row.
Dustbin of history, and being consigned to it.
Dynamic, as a noun.

E
Eatery.
Economics of the madhouse.
Edgy, to describe a work of art.
The elephant in the room.
Empower.
End of.
At the end of the day.
Enough already.
Envelope, except for stationery.
Epic fail.
Epicentre, except to mean the origin of
    an earthquake.
Epidemic of obesity, illiteracy, family
    breakdown or other social ills, which

are often 'reaching epidemic proportions'.

Ethnic, to mean non-white people, or pertaining to them, or to mean bohemian (also banned) or gypsy-like when referring to clothes or accessories.

'Events, dear boy, events.'

Every fibre of my being.

Evidence-based.

(All) the evidence tells us, to mean, 'I've read something about this somewhere that confirms my prejudices'.

'The exception that proves the rule', except when correctly used in legal argument (see page 36).

Exhibit a tendency to. One on George Orwell's list.

Existential. For example an existential crisis, meaning a serious one.

Exit strategy.

Expert. Banned from headlines; use elsewhere only with permission, which will not usually be granted.

Exponential or exponentially, to mean big or
a lot.

F
The fact of the matter is.
False dawn.
Famously. Or famous, when used thus: 'the
famous Hun, Attila'.
Fatally flawed.
Febrile. It means feverish.
Feisty. Like bubbly, always applied to women,
and therefore permitted only if referring to
heterosexual men.
Few and far between.
Finger pointing, usually 'I'm not going to get
into'.
Fingertip search.
Fine-tooth comb, and certainly not a fine
tooth-comb.
Fire the starting gun.
First priority (tautology).
(Not) fit for purpose, or unfit for purpose,
except when citing the Sale of Goods Act.

Flatlining, except to describe the vital signs
of dead people.

Fly in the face of.

Food chain, except to refer to animals that eat
other animals that eat plants.

Footfall. Inexcusable.

Foregone conclusion.

Foreground, as a verb.

Forget, at the start of a sentence or headline.
'Forget black, white is the new darkness.'
Sort of thing.

Forward planning, until the invention of a
time machine allows other kinds.

A forward policy. Or a forward offer.

Freebie.

Front line, or front-line. See back office.

Fuel, as a verb.

Full stops. When. Used. For. Emphasis.

G

Game changer, game-changing.

Game over.

Garner.

-gate, the suffix added to any news theme
supposedly embarrassing to the government.
Gateway.
Genie out of the bottle. It was a lamp, unless
you are from America, where the television
series *I Dream of Jeannie* may be as well
known as the original story.
Get one's head round something.
Get over it.
He/she gets it. They just don't get it.
The gift that keeps on giving.
Give rise to, or give grounds for.
Glaring loophole. How can a hole glare?
Go figure.
Go the extra mile.
Goalposts, moving of.
Going forward.
A good election to lose.
Graduate, except from university.
Granular, granularity, unless to do with
materials science.
Greater than the sum of its parts.
Grist to the mill.

Grind to a halt.

Ground-breaking: if it means the first dig
    at a construction site, why should it mean
    'innovative'?

Guarantees, cast-iron. Or copper-bottomed.
    Or not worth the paper they are written on.

H

Haircut, to mean a partial default on debt.
    It was vivid once, but it's wrong, because
    if you have your hair cut you lose a bit
    of hair about which you do not care; debt
    restructuring means bondholders lose
    actual money.

(All) the hallmarks of.

A hand up not a handout.

Hard wired, or hard-wire (verb).

Hard-working families.

Have the effect of.

A heads up.

Hearts and minds.

Heavy lifting.

Hey. This was the subject of a specific ban by

Simon Kelner, editor of *The Independent*.
    Worse is: 'But, hey.' Or 'hey ho.'
Hit the ground running.
Hoist with his own petard. Or 'by', although
    the original in *Hamlet* is 'with': a petard was a
    bomb carried by hand, with obvious dangers.
Hold fire.
Holed below the water line.
Holistic.
Hot-button issue.
Hotbed.
How I learned to stop worrying and
    (love the)…
Human shield.
Hymn sheet, singing from the same:
    sometimes secularised as 'song sheet'. Still
    unacceptable.

I
Iconic.
Ilk.
Impact, as a verb.
Implement, as a verb.

In intensive care, of a policy, especially one
     on healthcare.
In the mix.
In order to.
In relation to.
In respect of.
In spades.
In terms of.
Incentivise.
Inconvenient truth. This will presumably
     fade, along with the memory of Al Gore's
     2006 eco-apocalyptic documentary of
     that title.
Incredible or incredibly, as intensifiers.
Industrial, on an industrial scale, except when
     talking about factories.
Inextricably linked.
Instore (and even, I am told, 'inbranch', in
     some banks).
Interface. (A social networking question,
     according to Allan Christensen: Are you
     interfacebook?)
The introduction of.

Issues. There is always a better way. Especially
   if used to mean problems.

It's official.

It's the economy, stupid. Or it's anything else,
   stupid.

It's the *X* Wot Won It. ('It's *The Sun* Wot
   Won It' was the *Sun* front-page headline
   on 11 April 1992, the Saturday after the
   election, on the day of which Neil Kinnock
   had featured in a light bulb).

J

Job of work.

Joined-up government. Or joined-up thinking.

Joked (for said).

A journey, when not describing travel.

The jury is out, except in court reporting.

K

Key, adjective. Especially keynote speech. Or
   as a predicative, as in 'forward planning is
   key'.

Kick start, especially talks.

Killer app.

Killer fact.

Knows where the bodies are buried.

L

Landmark, except to describe something that
can be seen for miles.

Last ditch. Or last-ditch.

Last time I looked. Or checked. As in, 'Last
time I checked, Northern Ireland was part
of the United Kingdom.'

Learning curve.

We will take no lessons from *x* on *y*. Or lectures.

The level of.

Level playing field.

Level up, not down.

Leverage, as a verb. See also 'deleverage'.

On life support. See also: in intensive care,
especially of policies on the NHS.

Lifestyle.

Line in the sand. See 'draw'.

Living in the real world. See 'real world', and
the 'real people' who live there.

Living the dream.
Long grass, as a place into which to kick
    problems. And its American equivalent,
    'kick the can down the road.'
Low-hanging fruit.

M
Make contact with.
Make no mistake.
Makeover.
Man up.
A marathon, not a sprint.
Max out (the credit card).
Meet with.
Meritocracy. A word invented by Michael
    Young to describe an undesirable future in
    which clever people monopolise wealth and
    power.
Metric, noun, to mean a measure of progress.
Milestone. ('Like a gallstone, only bigger
    and more painful,' according to Allan
    Christensen.)
Militate against.

Mission, except in a religious or military sense.
  See passion and vision.
Moment in the sun.
Moment in time.
Moniker.
Mood music.
Moral compass.
Move on (from).
Move the goalposts.
A must read, or must-read as an adjective.
My bad. I did not believe that people could
  either say it or write it. Then it was on
  Doctor Who.

N
Name and shame.
Natch (short for naturally). It was archly witty
  in 1982.
National treasure, to refer to an entertainer
  who has been popular for some time.
Neglect *x* at our peril.
Newbie.
No ifs or buts.

No longer. Following a loving description
   of The Way We Were.

No mean achievement.

A no-brainer.

Normalcy.

Not, as in 'Something, not the opposite
   of something.' A New Labour favourite:
   'Forward, not back.'

Not a good look, applied to anything other
   than someone's physical appearance.

Not fit to clean/lick the boots of. Has been
   used by Christopher Hitchens, but, as he
   said, nobody is perfect.

Doing nothing is not an option. Of course it is; it
   is just not the option preferred. See status quo.

Nothing ruled out. Or in. 'I rule nothing out.'
   'Or in.'

Now, at the start of headlines, as in 'Now You
   Pay for Prison Parties' (*Daily Mail*, 26 July
   2010).

Now is not the time for.

Now more than ever.

O

Outcomes, such as 'learning outcomes'.

One-size-fits-all.

Ongoing.

Opening salvo.

Opine.

Organic, except to refer to farming or to the chemical science that deals with carbon-based compounds.

(Think) outside the box. Or out of the box.

Overarching.

P

Package, to mean television report. Used by television journalists and occasionally by studio guests trying to sound knowledgeable on programmes such as *Newsnight*.

A package of. Especially measures.

Panacea. Always 'Not a'.

Par for the course. Except in golf.

Paradigm. Especially paradigm shift and paradigmatic.

Parameter. Often plural and narrow. It is a

mathematical oxymoron, a constant that can
be varied, not another word for perimeter.

Park (an issue).

Participate. 'Take part in' will usually do.
Participation is also suspect.

Passion. See mission and vision. 'I am
passionate about' is unacceptable.

Passport, as a verb.

Pathway.

Pay down (debt). It should be 'repay' or
'pay off'.

Pen, as a verb. Especially as most people type
these days.

(Not) a penny piece.

Beyond peradventure.

Perfect storm.

Piece, to mean article. Often used by print
journalists of their own work, or by people
wishing to ingratiate themselves with the
same.

Pipe dream.

Place, as in 'in a good/bad place', to describe
someone's mental state.

Plan B.

Play a leading part (role) in. One of George
Orwell's 'verbal false limbs'.

Play into the hands of.

Playbook, as in 'the New Labour playbook'.
Covered by the blanket ban on American
sporting metaphors (a playbook is the list
of planned plays in American football,
which can run to hundreds of pages), but
deserves a listing of its own.

Plethora.

Political football.

Postcode lottery.

Pot, kettle.

Pre-prepare, pre-order, pre-book and the rest.
I lost an argument with Daniel Finkelstein
about the stickers brought in for London mini-
cabs a few years ago, which say 'Pre-Booked
Only'. I thought this was an acceptable
adaptation of English and that it was easier to
grasp than 'Booked Only'. He put me right.

Presses all the right buttons.

Preternatural.

The price of everything and the value
of nothing.
Prior to.
Prioritise.
Proactive.
Problematic, or, worse, problematise.
Progressive. It was on George Orwell's list too.
The prospect of.
Proverbial.
Psychodrama, to describe any tense political
relationship.
Pull out (all) the stops.
Pushing the envelope.

Q
Quantum. Such as 'financial quantum', which
James Murdoch said in his evidence to
the Home Affairs select committee, 19
June 2011; realising what he was saying,
he translated it as 'cost'. Murdoch also
said: 'There are thresholds of materiality,
if you will, whereby things have to move
upstream.'

Quantum leap, except to refer to a change in
    the quantum state of an electron.
Question mark over. Question marks go at the
    end, not above.
Quipped (for said).

R
Radar, to be or not to be on someone's; or to
    be 'under the'.
A raft of.
A range of.
Rank hypocrisy (or breathtaking).
Reach out.
Read across, noun.
Real people in real communities in the real
    world. In real time.
Rear-view mirror, except in cars.
Re-booting anything that isn't a
    computer.
Reclaim the language of.
Reconnect with the voters (or just connect
    with them, usually by articulating an
    overarching vision).

Red lines, which governments or parties will
  not cross in negotiations.
Red tape.
Reinvent the wheel.
Relationship between the individual and the
  state. Meaningless guff.
Render inoperative.
Resile. Posh way of saying 'retreat' or 'withdraw'.
Resonate, except when discussing the physics
  of a singer breaking a wine glass without
  touching it.
Retrofit, except in engineering.
Ride roughshod over.
Ring-fence.
Ring the changes.
Road map, except the kind made redundant by
  sat nav.
Robust, when used to describe data, policies
  or procedures.
(It's not) rocket science.
Rod for (someone's) own back.
Roll out, except carpet, wallpaper or logs.
Rookie. First-year professional sportsman

or woman. Covered by blanket ban on
American sporting metaphors.
Root and branch.
Rude awakening.
Rude health (the meaning of rude as 'vigorous,
robust' survives only in this phrase).
Running commentary, as in 'I'm not going to
give a', by someone not answering a question.

S

Sand, draw a line in the.
Same page, to be on the. Although the older
'on the same wavelength' deserves to survive,
as it suggests two parties being attuned to
each other.
Satire died when …
-scale, as in 'wide-scale', 'mass-scale' or even
'huge-scale', the last of which has been used
by Peter Oborne of the *Daily Telegraph*,
who has written books with footnotes and
who should know better.
Scant comfort.
Scion.

Scot free.

Sea change.

Seal the deal.

See what I/he/she did there?

Seed corn money. As in, 'You won't seed that
   again.'

Seismic shift.

Sell-by date. Except on perishable goods.

A sense of.

A series of.

Seminal. A favourite in TV culture shows, as
   in 'Tarantino's seminal *Reservoir Dogs*'.

Serve the purpose of.

Sex, lies and ... (insert your object of choice).

Shelf life.

Shocked and appalled.

Shred of credibility.

The silent majority (speaking up for).

Silos, except for grain or missiles.

Silver bullet, usually, like a panacea, noting the
   absence thereof: 'There is no silver bullet.'

Sing from the same hymn sheet.

Siren voices. Always trying to persuade

politicians to do things that they have no intention of doing, but can then mention to show how brave they are in ignoring them.

Skillset. (Has to be one word to capture its full horror.)

Skyrocket.

Sleaze.

Sleepwalking into (some undesirable state).

Smarts. Dying out, I hope.

Smoking gun.

Snatch victory from the jaws of defeat. Or vice versa.

Sneak peek.

So, at the start of an article. 'And so' is worse. 'And so it begins' is worst.

Soap opera, except to mean television drama serial (originally with a lot of washing powder advertisements in the breaks).

Social mobility. Sounds good but describes different, complicated and mutually incompatible things. Better to say what you mean.

Something of a.

So(u)briquet.

Spark, as a verb. Almost always a damp squib
as a metaphor.

To speak to … as a supposedly elevated way
of saying 'to talk about' or 'to comment on'.

Speak truth (un)to power.

Spiral of decline: often a downward spiral.

Spiral out of control.

Square the circle: a geometry task that is
regarded as impossible, although that
depends on how precise you want to be.
Anyway, it is a cliché.

Stakeholder. Unless you mean a zombie with
a pointed stick (one of Allan Christensen's
translations of local government
bureaucratic jargon).

Stalemate. Often a mistaken metaphor for a
long-lasting deadlock: in chess, stalemate is
a kind of draw; at my level, the result of a
mistake by the stronger player in failing
to allow his opponent any legal moves; at
higher levels, often forced by an apparently
weaker player in order to escape defeat.

Either way, it is the end of the game. It
follows, therefore, that you cannot 'break'
a stalemate.

Stand shoulder to shoulder with, except in
police line-ups.

Stark contrast.

State of the art.

The status quo is not an option. Likewise
'doing nothing'.

Step change.

Step forward, as in, 'How did the Banned List
take over the world? Step forward, John
Rentoul.'

Step up to the plate. Particularly silly in
Britain, as it is a baseball term.

Stinging attack or criticism.

Stop in its tracks.

Storyline, or any other unsuitable noun as a verb.

Strategic. Except in discussing how wars are
won or lost.

(Be) subjected to.

(Greater than) the sum of its parts.

Swan song.

Swingeing cuts.

Synergy, synergism, except in pharmacology or
physiology.

Systemic, especially failure.

T

Take effect.

Take forward.

Take on board.

Take up the cudgels for.

Talismanic.

Tangled web.

Team X. As in Team Cameron, Team Boris,
Team Ed.

Tectonic plates, except for earthquakes,
volcanoes and continental drift.

Territory, comes with the.

Text-message abbreviations: BTW, IMO,
IMHO, LOL, ROFL, TBH and so on. I
mean, whose opinion is it going to be?

Thank you for your patience. Or co-operation.

'They came', at the start of a news report.

Think outside the box.

Third person, referring to oneself in the.
Anything involving ticking and boxes.
(Ticking) time bomb.
Time critical, meaning urgent.
Time horizon.
(Only) time will tell.
Tin, does what it says on the.
Tipping point.
Tome.
Toolkit, unless it has a spanner in it.
Top-down.
Top priority (tautology again).
Touch base.
Tough love.
Toxic, except to describe a poison.
Trojan horse.
The truth is, before the peddling of
    an opinion.
Turkeys voting for Christmas.

U
Über.
UK plc.

Up and down the country. Or length and
     breadth of.

Upcoming. Foster Winans, a correspondent
     of mine, says that Bernard Kilgore, editor
     of the Wall Street Journal 1941-67, hated
     the word so strongly that, after seeing it in
     a published story one time too many, he
     sent a memo to the staff on the lower floor
     warning, 'The next time I see "upcoming"
     in the newspaper I will be downcoming and
     someone will be outgoing.'

Urban, when used to mean lots of foreigners
     or non-white people. See vibrant.

Utilise, forbidden when 'use' will do, which is
     always.

U-turn, as a verb.

V

Vibrant, when used to mean lots of foreigners
     or non-white people. See urban.

Vicious circle.

A victory for common sense.

Virtuous circle.

Vision. See mission and passion.

W
Wake-up call.
Wall of money.
Wall of silence.
War of words.
Way beyond, or way more. (Should be 'far'.)
We are all x now. Where x can be anything
    from Thatcherites to fashion icons.
We are where we are.
Weasel words.
Weather conditions.
A week is a long time in politics. Or variants
    thereof, such as, 'If a week is a long time in
    politics then a month seems an eternity.'
Well-oiled machine.
The Westminster village. Like 'inside the
    Beltway', which is now usually shortened to
    just 'Beltway', in America. This is sometimes
    shortened to 'the village'. I've used it myself.
    Time to pull the ladder up behind me.
What a difference a day makes. From a song

originally called 'What a Diff'rence a Day
Made'.

What's not to like?

Where someone is coming from. As in, 'I see
where you are coming from.'

Whisper it.

Who knew?

Win-win. Allan Christiansen suggested
that this is another way of saying 'a draw'.
If only.

Window, except to refer to a hole in a wall
with glass in it.

Without fear or favour.

Work hard and play by the rules, as in, 'people
who', or, worse, 'families who', with whom
politicians seek to reconnect. See 'hard-
working families.'

Wow factor, or any other factor, except in
mathematics.

Y

You couldn't make it up. (You usually could.)

Your call is important to us.

Z
Zero-sum game.

2.0, unless it refers to actual software.

20:20 hindsight. As in: 'With 20:20 hindsight and all that has followed, I would not have offered him the job.' David Cameron, referring to Andy Coulson, his former communications director (20:20 vision, or 20/20, refers to a standard opticians' test for good sight in both eyes at 20 feet).

24/7.

All words and phrases in foreign or dead languages. (Should 'blanket ban' be on the List? Perhaps not yet.) This means *alma mater*, etc (this is usually unnecessary, but if it is 'and so on' suffices), but it does not mean words which are assimilated into English *and* which have a useful and distinct meaning, such as cliché, vice versa, referendum. And so on.

All American sporting metaphors (for example, step up to the plate, ballpark, Hail Mary pass). British ones are bad enough, but at least most of us know what they mean.

ACKNOWLEDGEMENTS

I have learned from my colleagues at *The Independent* titles, including John Mullin, editor of *The Independent on Sunday*, who can spot a lazy phrase trying to hide sloppy thinking from accross the office; Simon Kelner, the former editor-in-chief, who used to move the 'onlys' in my leading articles to the right place until I learnt how to do it myself; Amol Rajan, an editor on the comment desk who took to Twitter to campaign for the use of 'moreover' and against tautology; and Guy Keleny, whose 'Errors & Omissions' column on Saturdays is one of the best things in the newspaper.

Matthew Parris and Paul Flynn, his producer at the BBC, generously gave me the list of 'Political

Deadspeak' that they compiled for a Radio 4 programme called *Not My Words, Mr Speaker*, in September 2007. Toby Young drew my attention to Graydon Carter's list of words banned from *Vanity Fair*, which Young reproduced in his excellent book, *How to Lose Friends and Alienate People*. Allan Christiansen from New Zealand emailed me his translations of 'corpolingo': words and phrases that had all been used by Auckland Council, for which he worked.

Olivia Bays at Elliott and Thompson contacted me after seeing my original Banned List on *The Independent* blog and suggested it should be a book. She used to work at the Commission for Racial Equality (now the Equality and Human Rights Commission), so she knows something about jargon. She improved an early draft by ordering me to be more judgemental. I am grateful for her enthusiastic support for the idea, and for the inclusion of impact (as a verb), natch, smarts and strategic.

Thank you all. Natch.

ABOUT THE BLOG

The Banned List in blog form can be found at www.bannedlist.co.uk

It continues to expand and the Committee stands ready to consider new additions. Readers are invited to send in their submissions via the blog or on Twitter using the hashtag #bannedlist

ABOUT THE AUTHOR

John Rentoul heads the committee that maintains the Banned List – his ever-growing collection of over-used, meaningless and offensive words and phrases. He is also chief political commentator for *The Independent on Sunday*, and visiting fellow at Queen Mary, University of London, where he teaches contemporary history. Previously he has worked for the BBC and *New Statesman*, and on an oil rig in the North Sea.